Secrets of Prosperity

Secrets of Prosperity

A SPIRITUAL BOOT CAMP

Mary Beth Murawski
and Jaime J. Harris

Focus Management Publications
New York
2002

ISBN: 0-9718387-1-2

Library of Congress Catalog Number: 2002106994

Edited by: Cambridge Literary Associates
Cover Design: Carrie Zeidman, Elan Studios
Layout Design: Ken Shelton, PEI

Published by

Focus Management Publications,
345 East 37th Street,
New York, New York, 10016
USA

focusmgt@aol.com

Printed in Canada

Dedication

This book is dedicated to:
Memé and Pepé, Edmund P. Gillis and Adele Gillis.
Pepé...for his simple teaching of the power of God at a young age. Thank you for the lesson about
Langueur, chère petite fille...slow down my little one.
And to my Memé...who taught me that all there is to life is love...nothing else matters.

M.B.M.

To the readers for their courage to embrace change, and the willingness to accept the outcome. And to Dolly Levi for her truism that, "Money is like manure – you have to spread it around and watch it grow."

J.J.H.

Contents

Real faith has a vision that can never be altered, interrupted or changed, unless God decides otherwise.

Mary Beth Murawski

Play It Forward

Have you ever noticed how people who achieve major success accept it so humbly, almost as if they expected it to happen? Did you ever wonder how it is that some people from the minute they open their eyes in the morning, seem to know exactly what they want and what to do to make it happen? If you listen to successful athletes or movie stars when winning awards and races, they are excited and happy yet they are rarely surprised by their achievements. You hear them talk about concentration, confidence and faith. But how do you train in confidence and faith? This is why we put together a spiritual boot camp called *Secrets of Prosperity*. This program is the basic training for abundant success and permanent prosperity in all areas of your life.

We felt called to write a book that applies the universal divine laws of prosperity and abundance to your daily activities, and that will encourage you to achieve success. Our *secrets* deliver a code of truth that will tease you into making changes in your life. *Secrets of Prosperity* is a toolbox of universal divine laws for everyday use.

Let's start by asking a very important question: what can I do right now, today, to reach my goals and become the prosperous, successful person I know I can be? The answer may surprise you. It begins with a challenge: you need to be willing and open to change your mind and to choose prosperity.

Our toolbox of activities is filled with what we call "mission steps," and you'll find them to be fun, creative and designed to fit into your daily routine. You will learn eleven simple yet profound lessons that will guide you to your heart's desires and limitless possibilities. We have faith that you will attain a sense of victory and fulfillment when you complete all eleven missions. We pray that all of you triumph over adversity as you move through each mission. We are confident in our message and its ability to bring you a joyful and abundant life. All you need is an ounce of faith, a touch of truth and a little eagerness.

In Boot Camp, you will discover your own natural ability to create within yourself what you desire in and around you. The missions will automatically open the flow of magical encounters for you.

As you begin to experience your own daily miracles, be aware of the synchronicities of people, places and events that enter your life. As human beings we all feel defeated at one time or another. You do not have to struggle with setbacks and feel resentment any longer. Do not let yourself remain preoccupied by problems, cares and difficulties. *Secrets of Prosperity* will reveal methods for channeling your spirit power through your thoughts and actions, thus canceling out all obstacles.

Our book will give you the, 'what, why and how' to living a prosperous life on a permanent basis. We suggest that you work *Secrets* for an entire ninety-day period. All phases work together to make a complete cycle as you integrate this program into your life. We thoroughly believe to the core of our souls that this book can improve your life immensely.

The *Secrets of Prosperity* ideas are not new but have been hidden. As a matter of fact, our research shows that as far back as Biblical times many of these Universal Laws were handed down to Abraham and Joseph as ageless wisdom. Schools of prosperity were established for the sons of the wealthy and noble. U.S. Anderson wrote in the *Three Magic Words* the following: "There have been besides Jesus, many enlightened men and societies who have lived on this planet. Yet these men and societies have thought it dangerous to reveal this knowledge to humanity as a whole." *Secrets* will reveal these same ancient laws but with modern techniques.

We deeply desire success for you and wish for you to be comfortable with our language. You will hear us refer to 'God' as our higher power. We invite you to substitute your own higher power's name. We are all spiritual beings. The power that creates us is the power that knows us.

The universal truth is, we are all part of God's divine universal substance. No one person, religion or ethnic background is more significant than any other. We are all one. We are all inter-connected. What happens to one affects all of us. We are all equally deserving of prosperity and abundance.

Rev. Paul Tenaglia, pastor of the Unity Church of New York City, says, "Universal Law is the law of divine principle that God is unchanging, eternal, invisible energy that keeps everything together in divine order, harmony, and love. Divine Law is the principle under which the universe exists. The law that keeps the planet and the stars in order, the law that keeps us grounded on earth, the law that says that every created being in the universe is supported, loved, and provided for simply because we are one with it."

According to the Universal Divine laws, it is our divine birthright to attain perfect health, unlimited wealth, and permanent prosperity. This ability to live a wholesome, productive life in peace without fear, guilt or shame, is our divine inheritance from birth as children of God.

You will learn that you are a rich child of Gods' divine creation and that you are a deserving child of God, regardless of your current circumstance in life.

According to the divine law doctrine, *Secrets of Prosperity* instructs on how to acquire the inherent divine energies (or spirit) within you. It shows you how to empower your emotional self by accepting and receiving from your divine inner source. You will learn to be the guardian of your world through the power of thought and words.

Secrets of Prosperity is derived from the universal divine laws of truth. James Allen sums it up by saying, "The world is your kaleidoscope, and the varying combinations of colors which at every succeeding moment it presents to you are the exquisitely adjusted pictures of your ever-moving thoughts."

We believe that the future of humanity depends on happy and healthy people like you to create prosperity for yourself. As you become truly abundant in all areas of your life, it will spread forward to people around you, and then to people around them, until we hold and sustain peace and prosperity in the hearts of all mankind. The world awaits your contribution as light workers of the 21st century! Welcome to Boot Camp!

With joy,
Mary Beth Murawski
Jaime J. Harris

Write It Down

The law of desire is: To achieve one's goals in life, one must desire them.

Faith concentrates on the journey with joy because it knows the results are already there.

Imagine that an angel appears to you right now and says, "I will grant your every dream, wish, need, desire or want."

Would you know what that would be? Could you answer the angel? Do you know what you want?

Many people do not get what they want because they do not know what they want. They only have a vague idea of their dreams and goals. Their vision of what they want changes almost daily and they never stay focused to achieve their heart's desires or dreams and goals.

This first step to receiving what you want out of life is very simple. Staggeringly simple. The first step is to write it down!

Write down what you want just like a shopping list. Declare what you want and then write it down. This can be anything. It could be a loving relationship, a fantastic career, financial independence, a college degree, perfect health or a beautiful new home.

Let your imagination take over without fear or doubt. This is not the time to think in practical terms or to be conservative. This list is for you only and not to be shared with anyone. So let yourself be as open and bold as you want to be. Remember, the question is if you could truly have anything...anything at all...what would that be?

The 'good life' you dream of...filled with comfort, safety, contentment and love, is the *good* that will appear once you start with writing down what you want. Obtain a notebook or blank book from a stationary store. Title it, *My Book.* This is your special book to write your daily missions that we will discuss in detail at the end of this chapter. This book is for your eyes only. Keep your *I want* list to yourself. Your special angel gives you permission to write with confidence and excitement expecting only the best. The *I want* list is different from a *to do* list. In a *to do* list you have focused activities that leave no room for the unexpected to happen, e.g., go to the store, pick up the laundry, etc.

Your *I want* list is the result of your dreams and desires taking shape as you write it down. For example, "I want the right and perfect career." Or "I want a dream vacation with that special person."

The Truth is: The life that you are living right now is the result of your own thoughts and belief systems.

The life that you are living right now is the direct result of your thoughts, your words, your actions and belief systems.

Sadly, some people do not acquire what they want in life because they believe they do not deserve to be rich, well or happy, or that they can achieve their dreams. If you believe you cannot have, then you will not have. You attract to yourself riches or poverty, sickness or health, joy or sadness, all according to the kingdom that you create within. If you constantly entertain thoughts of illness and weakness, then you will be ill or weak.

Many people I know have trouble just saying "I want success" without a guilt feeling. Your thoughts about what you deserve and your belief about what you can achieve can stop you from living an abundant life if you feel unworthy. Most people were brought up believing that 'to want' is to be greedy. Alternatively, that to be "poor in spirit" is righteous. The message in the Beatitudes is often misunderstood. To be poor in spirit means to be willing to empty your present habits of wrong thought, to remove your present attitudes and prejudices to make way for the divine to come in. Society teaches us that 'to want' is being materialistic...to be rich is to be a snob. But the truth is it is not a sin to desire financial independence, or to declare prosperity for your life. Your conscious mind and your higher self need to be told that it is OK to want the best for yourself, what ever that may be. You can arrive at success and receive whatever your heart desires. Add pure intention and faith to your thoughts and you will claim your desires on earth.

The truth is that when you have a yearning for something better in your life, it is your divine spirit whispering in your ear, reminding you of your true potential. All ideas are divine ideas that originate from your inner spirit. Your rational mind often stops you from getting what you want. Don't let it. You are in control.

That constant desire you call 'wishful thinking' nagging at you is God reminding you that you do have a greater purpose in this life. Real faith knows that we came here for a purpose and it is time to live that purpose here and now.

If you have a vague image of where you see yourself, then the universe will respond to you in vague, unclear ways. For example, I want to live in a new house someday. Without describing the new house in exact detail, you could end up with a house that is falling down. During my first move to Los Angeles, I drove down the Pacific Coast Highway. I found myself surrounded by the beauty and of Malibu. For just a moment, I wished that I could live in Malibu. That's all. It was a fleeting thought that was unclear. I left Los Angeles and returned eight years later. My wish came true.

I did end up living in Malibu, overlooking the ocean on the Pacific Coast Highway. Only it was a in one room flat attached to another apartment where a group of unsavory people lived in the room adjacent to me. I uncomfortably shared the bathroom with them. Yes, the universe responded to my thoughts many years later but with a vague, chaotic demonstration. I learned to be very clear and specific about the conditions of my home, and what I wanted it to look like from that point on.

We have five exercises that we will call MISSIONS. The following missions will become the Master Plan for your life. The first set of missions are writing drills designed to explore and identify your dreams and goals. As you write in long hand, you are turning off your mind chatter and turning to that secret place within. The secret place is your conscious mind, it is where your thoughts flow. You can claim power and dominion over that secret place inside when you merge with the divine consciousness: by being still and listening within.

'Mind Scientists' are researchers who are unfolding and discovering aspects of consciousness to get the best peak performance out of one's own mind. As brain cells become quieter as in meditation...the frequencies become lower. As the frequencies become lower, the amplitude becomes greater. Meaning the amplitude or the power of your thoughts becomes greater, as in turning up the volume. It appears that brain cells radiate electromagnetic energy in rhythmic patterns. These vary from one to more that forty hertz. The electromagnetic signature of 'thought', the regular thoughts you think, is around 15-16 HZ. In biofeedback studies the electromagnetic signature of 'attention,' as in when you put your attention to what you are writing down, begins at 13HZ (significantly lower) and include frequencies that are in the Alpha state. The Alpha state is the same electromagnetic brain wave pattern as in meditation. The implication here is that the 'attention' state is a superior form of thought. So the quieter the mind is, the greater the amplitude of the attention on your thoughts, thus the greater the impact on your brain.

When you write a thought on paper, your full attention is focused on that thought. Your mind cannot write one thought and think other thoughts at the same time. When you see on paper your heart's desires, in your own penmanship, you switch on the visualization department of your mind.

When you re-record your thoughts to prosperous abundant living, your mind will co-create what you record. It has to. Your mind will only do what you tell it. As you write down your lists of what you want your life to be, you are using three different cognitive techniques.

1. Slowing down the brain process to achieve full attention in the moment
2. Organization of a life plan
3. Visually recording to the subconscious exactly what you want.

Mission # One

Writing from the heart

The goal of this mission is to write down your heart's desires, wishes and dreams as asked to you by the angel. Everything and anything you want. Just write it down. Write for as long as you want. Be as detailed and as precise as you can. You should do this mission every day as early as possible for the next ten days. You may find that you enjoy writing from the heart and continue to do this mission after the ten days are up.

Get yourself comfortable in a seated position and have your notebook ready.

We suggest a one-minute meditation before you start your Heart Writing mission to enhance your attention state and to open your mind's eye to your true desires.

Light a candle and focus on the light around the glow of the flame. Breathe deep and slow ten times. Stare at the flame and memorize the shape. Close your eyes and just be still. Continue for one minute as you focus on clearing all thoughts. We suggest stating the following phrase:

I am one, I am...I am...I am, ...

I am one with the divine spirit.

By stating the *I am* mantra, you are connecting to the Almighty. Feel your body slowly and gently sink into a natural rhythm of your heart...begin now to write the desires of your heart.

Mission #2

The Quick List

For this mission you will write down quick thoughts and desires for two and a half minutes for the following categories:

Career　Relationships　Health
Financial　Family/Leisure

Take five blank separate pages...write at the top of each page those headings. At the top of page one, write the word 'Career' and then date the page. On the top of page two write 'Relationships.' On the top of page three write 'Health.' On the fourth page write 'Financial,' and on the fifth page write 'Family/Leisure.'

Now get out your watch and set it for two and one half minutes.

The goal of mission two is to write down what you want under the topic of 'career' within the two and a half minute time limit. Write down the ideas, images and thoughts surrounding the word 'career.' This mission is most effective when you stay within the two and half minute time limit. The purpose of the time line is to release the first thoughts that come to you surrounding each topic.

Next re-set your clock and write down what you want under 'relationships.' Quickly write whatever comes up. Include thoughts and phrases even if they do not relate to the topic. Write your desires for the right and perfect relationships or that special person within the two and half-minute period. Then onto page three, health. Page four is financial, and the last page is family/leisure.

After you compile your quick lists make sure you date the page. Later we are going to look at the list for the Master Plan. Keep all your lists together by that date. Please do this mission for ten days. Start out your day with your Heart Writing mission followed by the Quick List on the same day. For the first ten days, you have two missions a day. Have fun!

Mission #3

Master Plan

The Master Plan is your life plan, for the next five years. You will start by reviewing everything that you have written down in the last ten days. Find a space to spread out all ten days of mission number one and mission number two. Look at mission #1 Heart Writing, and compare it to the Quick Lists of the same day. Then examine each day's writing. Analyze and review each of the days, from the first to the tenth day. Are you vague and unclear in one or more categories? Have you been honest in your appraisal of your goals and dreams? Did you write down exclusively what you want as opposed to what others want for you? Use colored pencils to circle needs and goals that re-appear the most often. Use different colored pencils for mental changes, physical changes, financial changes, and health. For example, you could use green for financial changes and blue for career.

Can you see any breaks in your thoughts or vagueness with your desires from the Quick List to your Heart Writing? What did you want on one day that you overlooked two days later? What issue kept coming up for you daily? Notice what you want short term and then long term. Take note of those goals and desires that you want or need now and for the future. This process is truly eye opening. You will be able to identify and 'see' the desires that are held strongly in your heart.

Now that you have examined your desires of what you want your life to be, re-write every detail in a time line. You will organize your desires in a time line for one month, six months, one year, two years, and five years. After you have completed your Master Plan, each and every day you will re-read it. Reflect on your Master Plan. Make amendments and changes as they come up.

The purpose of the Master Plan is to keep your desires focused and organized. As you write down and reflect on your Master Plan daily, your mind will not sway from the truth of what you want. The most compelling action you can take to reach prosperity and daily abundance is to create a Master Plan for your life. When you complete your Master Plan, you will no longer have a vague or unclear image of your dreams and goals.

So now when your angel appears to grant your every wish, dream and desire you have it written in your Master Plan! Donald Trump is famous for writing down his goals and so should you!

Mission #4

Burn This

For this mission you will write down all the reasons why you THINK you cannot succeed. What is stopping you or what do you think is stopping you from obtaining your goals?

The Burn This mission is your Cinderella list. "I cannot go to the ball because I don't have a dress. I have to stay home and sweep the ashes. Who else will wash these floors but me? I am too short to ride in the pumpkin carriage! I cannot wear those shoes, my feet are swollen. And everyone has a fairy godmother but me." All of the excuses and reasons you think you must stay at home and not enjoy the ball of life, write it down. After you have the list with all the reasons why you cannot possibly succeed, burn the list. Let all the negative thoughts have their moment in print and then burn it. If you do not have a place to burn your list, then rip it up and flush it down the toilet. The royal flush goodbye!

Mission #5

Flash Movie

We all love to go to the movies. In this mission, you will be developing your creative imagination to make your own flash movie. A mental flash movie is using your mind's eye to create quick scenes that run like a movie in your mind. For example, see yourself prosperous, abundant and happy. Can you visualize and see yourself being rich, well and happy? Now keep that visual image in your mind and attach a mental flash feeling of permanent prosperity. See yourself rich, well and happy. What is the feeling you get deep in your gut? What expression do you hold on your face? Are you able to stay focused or does your mind wander?

Let's try another. See yourself at perfect peak health. Identify the feeling. What are you wearing? What is your face expressing? What are you doing?

Refer back to your Master Plan and 'flash image' yourself receiving all you have written down. As you create a mental flash movie, visualize yourself at your personal best, receiving your dreams come true. Make it as real as possible and live in the creative energy of the flash movie. It only takes a moment to see and feel the images of prosperity and success. Hold it in your mind for as long as you can. Allow movement in your flash movies. Create an entire scene for yourself. Go for the Academy Award (it's always good to think big).

Visualizing and formulating your inner requests is a dress rehearsal to receiving the real thing. The moment you can make the pictures in your mind 'real' is the very instant that it will become truth. Imagination is one of the greatest secret weapons for success. It is your sacred duty as a child of God to accept nothing but happiness and success. Make your present moment engulfed by your heart's desire. See yourself already receiving what you want by using the greatest tool, your imagination.

Notes on Mission One
Heart Writing

Doodle Space

Notes on Mission Two
The Quick List

Career

Relationships

Health

Financial

Family/Leisure

Notes on Mission Three
Master Plan

One Month

Six Months

Two years

Five Years

Doodle Space

Notes on Mission Four
Burn This

What is stopping me or what do I think is stopping me from obtaining my goals?

Doodle Space

Notes on Mission Five
Flash Movie

In your mind's eye, see yourself already receiving prosperity by visualizing your dreams in a mini flash movie.

Doodle Space

Doodle Space

Creating a Vacuum

"Faith is god in action and non-action at the same time."

Mary Beth Murawski

Now that you have your master life plan, you need to create an opening and make room for yourself to receive your dreams. Make your life ready to receive it. The universe will recognize the opening and fill it with abundance.

To create a vacuum in your life means to remove everything in your life that is stopping the flow of success, wealth, happiness, joy and creativity from coming to you.

There are three types of vacuums: A Physical Vacuum, a Social Vacuum, and a Mental Vacuum. When we remove the clutter in both our minds and in our physical surroundings, this ignites an opening to make way for the new *good* (what it is you want) to appear in your life.

The first is a Physical Vacuum. This is a bold and adventurous act and one that takes courage. The law of prosperity states that you must remove what you do not want in your life in order to create an opening for greater prosperity to come to you.

Begin to implement the law of prosperity by removing anything that you are no longer using to make room for what you do want. Identify everything that is creating clutter in your life, then simply remove it. Creating a Physical Vacuum in your life is much like a spring-cleaning of all your physical belongings. You need to get rid of everything that is hanging around in your closet, the garage, the storage shed, or in your basement that no longer serves you. The rule of thumb for physical objects or tangibles is if you have not used it in a year, discard it.

For example, if you would like to launch a new business go through your business files and papers and throw away all documents that no longer have meaning. This will magically make way for new and profitable business to come to you. If you desire new clothing, give away old clothes. If you desire new furnishings, donate your old furniture or have a yard sale.

Go through your closets and drawers. You can donate your clothes to the Salvation Army or a church charity. In most cases, you can get a tax deduction. New substances cannot flow to you in a cluttered situation. So toss out the clutter!

Ask a friend to help you on your mission to get rid of old stuff. You may never realize the sentimental attachments to your things until it is time to let go. For example, for years I carried around old tattered t-shirts with my college emblem on the front. The good old days of being in college were sentimental, yet I was broke in those good old days. Old employment documents are hard to throw away. Toss them out. Your ex lover left some personal items that you are holding onto for him/her. Get rid of them. The magazines you never read from last year, throw them out. Throw out photos of the person who broke your heart. Letting go of the old can only bring you closer to your greater *good*. This requires some risk taking and faith on your part. Remember, you are making room for your true abundance to appear. By creating a vacuum, this opens new space for you to receive.

I want to share with you a compelling story. Several years ago, I made a life changing decision. We owned two condominiums that overlooked the World Trade Center.

The view from the top of the units was spectacular. We could not decide whether to rent or to sell. One day my intuition guided me to read a real estate brochure in the pile of mail. In the past I always threw away junk mail. However, that particular day I was guided to call this real estate agent regarding the potential sale of the two condominiums. The agent came over that afternoon with such enthusiasm and possibility. We decided to sign the contract with Ellison to represent the sale of condominiums. Although we were not ready for the sale, we decided to sign it, just to see what would happen. It all happened so fast.

First, we gave thanks to God in advance for the right and perfect people to buy the units. Then we began to create a vacuum in both the units. Like a tornado, we went through the place. Daily we removed two or three oversized trash bags of collected stuff that no longer was serving us. Every day in full faith we packed away dishes and books as if we were ready to move. We packed up clothing and gave to charity those items that no longer served our new lifestyle.

It was very emotional for us to let go of personal items, yet we remained completely focused on our goal. We wrote down the exact amount of money that we wanted to receive from the sale. We put in writing that we wanted both units to sell before ninety days were up. We further wrote down that we wanted the units to sell within two weeks of each other. We packed everything up as if the moving truck was downstairs ready to be loaded. We fixed and painted the units to look immaculate. When nighttime came, with boxes all around us, we visualized in faith the perfect sale. More importantly, we "visually visited" our new home on the ocean for at least a half hour before retiring. We always gave thanks in advance for the right and perfect sale. Every morning we continued to create a Physical Vacuum by packing away furniture, dishes, and business equipment. When potential buyers walked through, our units were spotless. Our broker commented that she wished we had more units for her to sell as we made it so easy for her to show.

Because of faith and our daily vacuums, the two condominiums sold within the ninety days and they were the highest selling units in the history of our neighborhood. They also sold within a week of each other! The vacuum process works!

The Social Vacuum is when you lovingly release the people in your life who are no longer supporting your growth. This sounds extreme at first, but surrounding yourself with people who may harbor resentment or have an aversion to you becoming successful, will stop you from achieving your goals. Silently bless those people, thank them for the lessons you have learned, and allow them to move onto their greater good. That is all you have to do. We do not suggest that you must make a formal declaration for someone to get out of your life. Just bless the person silently and thank them for the lessons you have learned together. Silently pray for them to find their greater *good* in life and to find happiness. This silent blessing will release anyone from limiting your belief in yourself. Become aware of your relationships. One day you will look around and notice that you have attracted new kindred spirits who support your prosperity belief system.

If a particular person is talking negativity around you with judgment about others, bless that person with an affirmation to generate their good elsewhere. Silently say,

I bless you for the goodness in you as I no longer respond to gossip and negativity.

If a friend or associate tells you that you will never measure up to your dreams, just allow that person to find their own path and let God and the universe do the rest. If someone speaks wrongly against you then silently bless that person.

I bless you for the goodness in you that you find your greater good as I move onto to my greater good.

Ask yourself is there wrong conduct anywhere in my thoughts? Do I continue to judge or condemn others? In order for the good to manifest in your life, you need to remove the negative blocks within your own mind. Some people have a curious habit of not wanting others to achieve a higher path in life. There are those who consciously or unconsciously wish for others not to be successful. They simply have not come to the truth that there is plenty for everyone. This is a rich and generous universe and there is plenty for everyone! Remove all that clutters your life both physically and socially to make way, in faith, to receive your good.

The third vacuum is called a Mental Vacuum. This will be the removal of well-hidden and deep-rooted negative beliefs systems about yourself. You will begin to notice these negative patterns when you begin *Secrets of Prosperity*. Negative thoughts like, "I cannot do this, or who am I to desire prosperity?" Emotional patterns of negative thoughts are stuck deep within our mental blueprint. A subconsciously embedded negative belief system can create the stress associated with feelings of lack and limitation. To combat negative beliefs that appear as mind chatter, we find that discipline is not enough.

Make a commitment right now to change your thoughts at the deepest level of your mind. You can change your life by changing your thoughts. The subconscious always overrides the conscious mind and is a much stronger motivating force than self-discipline or will power.

If we desire one thing consciously and the opposite keeps appearing, then our needs or requests do not conform to our subconscious beliefs. Therefore, we must replace deep thoughts and beliefs of lack and limitation, sickness, fear or resentment, in the subconscious mind with new and more constructive positive thoughts. In Boot Camp, this is the war, the conscious desires vs. the subconscious programmed images and thoughts. Many people become angry or depressed over their lack of self-discipline.

We have all heard people say; "I have no self-discipline that is why I pick up a drink...eat a piece of cake...or go into rage. I can't get anything done. I have no self-discipline!"

Your self-discipline is being overridden by your subconscious mind. The secret here is to flood your subconscious mind with new pictures, new thoughts and new words about yourself in a positive way.

You have already started the process of changing your subconscious negative beliefs at the subconscious level when you wrote in Mission #1 and visualized in Mission #5. With the flash movie, you started changing your subconscious mind. Each mission from now on will implement the process of flooding your sub-conscious.

Bad mental habits are filled with extraordinary potency. Use the Mental Vacuum mission to catch yourself when you start to put yourself down. "I must be a dummy" or "I am too fat" or "I am too old."

This is the time to stop the mental gymnastics in your mind and ask the questions: who, what, when, why and how?

Pause and ask yourself the following:

Who taught me this thought?

What triggered this thought?

When did I first hear this thought?

Why did I choose to own this thought?

How can I get rid of this thought?

Understand and change your mind. Vacuum out all old thoughts of your destructive self and put in new *I want* thoughts that will empower you. Negative thoughts that no longer serve you must be removed by a vacuum.

Creating a vacuum is one of the most compelling and effective ways to initiate and maintain permanent prosperity and abundance in all areas of your life. As the superconscious mind merges with your own divine mind within, the results will be nothing short of miraculous.

Notes on: Physical, Social and Mental Vacuum

Physical Vacuum

Social Vacuum

Mental Vacuum

Doodle Space

Affirmations

"Our faith grows as we stretch forth our ability to become aware...and to observe the moment completely."

Mary Beth Murawski

Make a habit of thinking prosperous thoughts. The spoken word has suggestive power that reaches the inner psyche of the mind. Words are more powerful than thought. The spoken word is dynamic in nature because words literally can create. Whatever you affirm aloud becomes the manifestation of your reality. Be careful of what you say because it will eventually come true!

By affirming, you are making what it is that you desire...firm. State the following affirmation aloud: *I am rich, well and happy and all of my affairs are in divine order now.*

Every day you use affirmations when you speak your thoughts and feelings. Here is a little skit of a negative affirmative dialogue.

MB: "Hello, Jaime. How are you today?"

JH: "Hi, I am lousy thanks."

MB: "What's wrong?"

JH: "I don't know. Everything."

MB: "What do you mean? Like what?"

JH: "My boss is mad at me. My bird is sick. My feet hurt and I am miserable."

MB: "Well, you look good."

JH: "I do! Gee, I feel tired."

MB: "You got your hair cut. It looks cute."

JH: "Really? I hate it. I hate everything."

MB: "You have new sneakers... nice."

JH: "Oh, I'll trip over these just the same."

In the above dialogue, Jaime affirmed exactly what her world will produce. Most people do not realize how negative their words are. Make an observation of your conversations with people and count how many times you respond in a negative way. You might be surprised, even shocked, at the numbers you come up with!

The power of the spoken word was used for healing thousands of years ago. Ancient civilizations used the spoken word in various chants for their healing methods. Many ancient civilizations such as the Egyptians, the Greeks, and the Persians used the power of affirmations to create.

These affirmations and chants brought healing and power to their decrees, which raised the vibrational forces of man. So *Affirmations* can also be described as "scientific prayer" or a "spiritual treatment."

Here are several affirmations that I use on a daily basis.

I am the perfect child of God.

I am perfect health, wealth and success now.

I live in lavish abundance now as my body, my mind and emotions are healed right now.

Perhaps your prayers or dreams have not been obtained simply because you have not "asked" for then affirmatively. Affirmations are also known as spiritual decrees.

Job 22: 28 states, "Thou shall decree a thing and it shall be established unto thee and light shall shine upon thy ways."

Here is a great affirmation that works wonders when you start your day:

Today I am filled with creative loving energy, and I am a magnet to success!

By speaking aloud, you hear yourself making firm or solid your desire and send your intention or desire out to the divine universal intelligence to bring it forth. Words move in the ethers of creation to form the exact right condition described for it to manifest from the God intelligence of the universe. By speaking aloud exactly what you need or want in the form of an affirmation, you increase the rate of manifestation of your desire. Remember, your conscious mind will only bring forth and deliver to you the words and the solutions that you tell it.

The goal in this mission is to develop and write your own affirmations. You will describe in detail what you want and just simply speak the words into reality. Remember the categories in phase one: Career, Relationships, Health, Finances, and Family/Leisure? Refer to what you wrote down in phase one of *Secrets* as well as your Master Plan. Your tools are your words by which you create your life. Begin now to write out affirmations that will enable your dreams, goals or desires to become reality. Use words, thoughts and phrases that resonate with your own truth.

Here are some samples for you to begin:

I am receiving.

I am receiving all the love God wants me to give.

I am permanently prospered now.

I am surrounded by abundance and prosperity always.

When you state *I Am* verbally, this merges with the Christ consciousness or the divine universal flow and delivers your good according to the words you speak. *I AM* was the Hebrew name for God for good. The secret here is to use the power of the *I am* at either the beginning or at the end of your affirmation

I am a brilliant and successful________________

I am, I am, I am.

I am a loving and respected______________________

I am, I am, I am.

I am beautiful, peaceful and poised________________

I am, I am, I am.

I am one with divine wisdom___________________

I am, I am, I am.

Today, I am successful in_______________________

I am, I am, I am.

As you write your own affirmations, and as you prosper in your life, most of your thoughts and your words will become a living affirmation. When doing your affirmations ask with glory, praise and thanksgiving. Ask with passion and expect the results to appear!

You might feel shy or embarrassed about stating your wants, needs and desires out loud. Most people do. But as you exercise this mission each day, you will become more and more confident in your ability to call forth your dreams. Go to a place where you can really state your affirmations aloud. An open field is great, or even while you are driving in your car. Instead of singing in the shower, speak your affirmations with conviction, truth and belief. There is no need to feel shy or embarrassed. After all, as a child of God, there is absolutely nothing wrong with wanting only good things in your life.

A person with a rich consciousness attracts riches. A person with a poor consciousness attracts poverty. By your word, spoken aloud, you contact the divine power within you, which in turn promptly removes burdens, and you become free. You can begin to revolutionize your life through prayers of affirmations. Words spoken aloud help one to tap into all the power of the universe. God's power.

I am no longer in lack or limitation.

Everything is perfect now. Thank you, God.

Divine guidance prospers me now.

I can do all things through Christ who strengthens me.

Success comes to me quickly and with ease.

The spoken word also removes old negative thoughts that have crowded your mind and emotions. All of your negative thoughts need to be emptied. As you empty your mind and emotions of wrong thought you become purified. As you articulate your affirmations (stating verbally whatever you want), the words will dissolve blocks or obstacles.

Today I give up all fear and accept lavish abundance now.

I forgive myself. I love myself.

I let go of past pain. I live in joy today.

All fear, resentment, anger and guilt are removed with blessings. For example, if a circumstance or situation does not happen as you had hoped, then look for where you might have been resentful or unhappy. Then affirm a blessing of the event or situation. When anger, hurt or resentments are removed, you will be given the desire of your heart. This is divine law, which is immutable.

Have you ever been wronged or hurt by someone you love? Of course you have. We all have. Try stating the following:

I bless you for the good you have brought into my life and I forgive you.

For example, if you were fired from your job, state the following:

I bless my time with you and the lessons I have learned.

If you have had a misunderstanding with a friend, try affirming:

All is forgiven between us. I bless you on to your higher good as I move forward into my greater good.

You are afraid you will not get the acting part. Let go of the worry:

All fear is false. I now merge into oneness with God as I am blessed in all ways right now. I give praise and thanksgiving for my lessons learned.

Once you have made up your own powerful affirmations record them on a tape recorder. In the evening before you retire, play your tape and allow it to continue even after you fall asleep. Listen to yourself affirm your desires quietly. Your words will go directly to your higher self as you drift off to sleep. George Burns listened to his own personal affirmations every evening. He continued to perform and entertain with charm well into his nineties!

Here are just a few samples for you to record and listen to before retiring in the evening:

God is with me and I cannot fail.

I am blessed in all areas of my life. I am. I am. I am.

The right and perfect people are coming into my life now.

I am a loving and deserving child of God.

I bless this warm, comfortable home.

I am a magnet to success and abundance.

Everything prospers me now.

You can also attach a flash movie to your affirmations. Use the same format that we showed you earlier in the *Write it Down* section. This way you can implement the power of visual imaging along with the power of the spoken word.

The right and perfect job is coming to me.

I give thanks for my new job.

For an athlete:

My eye is on the ball.

My body is moving perfectly and with power as I hit the ball.

See yourself delivering a perfect performance. Thank you, God.

As we begin to experience positive results from our daily affirmations, situations and people will begin to resonate and mirror your zest for life. You will have peace, joy and a new sense of well-being. Speak forth your prayers of decrees daily at regular intervals. Be consistent and firm with your affirmations. Repeat the same affirmations until your prayers are answered.

There is an old saying that man only dares to use words for three reasons; to "bless, heal, or to prosper." What man says to others will in turn be said of him, and what he wishes for another, he seeks for himself.

Additional affirmations you can use:

All of my affairs are in divine order now.

All the energy that God created in the universe works in and through me today.

Divine guidance shows me the right and perfect way.

I am surrounded by a band of angels, who will show me the right and perfect way.

Doodle Space

Forgiveness: The Freedom Tool

"Faith just is"
Mary Beth Murawski

As you discovered in the vacuum mission, it is difficult to let new substance flow to you when there is clutter around you. This clutter can also be old anger, resentment, fear of someone, fear of success or failure, or the past pain of a relationship gone wrong. Make a commitment to yourself right now to freely release and let go of all negativity, fear, resentment and chaos in your life.

Forgiveness means to give up. To give up: old feelings, old attitudes and past bitterness. With our past all forgiven, we keep our full attention on today. Our today is where we create our tomorrows. The past is a mere guideline for the lessons we have learned. Today's thoughts and words are the actions of tomorrow. Forgiveness helps us to live in love in the present moment. Real forgiveness is the freedom to love.

When you are experiencing lack or limitation in one or more areas of your life, there is a good chance that you need to forgive someone or something. Forgiveness starts with forgiving yourself. Forgiveness is the mental liberation that frees us. When we do not practice forgiveness in our lives, it fosters anger, resentment and grows into hate. When we hold onto the incident that caused us pain, it short-circuits our ability to receive peace and prosperity.

Oftentimes we feel that others have "wronged" us unjustifiably and that we have done nothing erroneous or wrong to create the incident. No matter how well you can rationalize that you are right in a situation or conflict, or that you have been wronged by people, places or things, the truth is you are hurting yourself by not forgiving, releasing and letting go. Even if you are right. Forgive anyway, regardless of who or what the circumstance is. At the same time, the person in conflict will also subconsciously be released and freed.

The person, event, or situation is a lesson in your life that has done its teaching. Forgive and move on. Discover your good elsewhere. The unforgiving person hangs onto the old pain of being right. Holding resentments causes ill health, depression, sickness, lack, limitation, and sometimes even poverty.

The greatest fear that we have as human beings is to be abandoned by someone we love. Well, that is what happened to me. For reasons known to God only, a man that I loved and supported, mentally and financially, left me without a note or notice back in 1991.

I was left waiting for him for three hours at the boat dock in Woods Hole after a day's work...he never arrived to pick me up in my car.

I found out later that he had packed everything from our apartment including the bank account and left the country. Never to be seen or heard from again. Words cannot describe how I felt. I was hurt, enraged and rejected. How did this happen to me? With no warning. Gone. If any of you have had a broken heart, you know the pain. From that moment on, I lost trust. I resented this man for many years. Three months later, the other man in my life died, my father. I went deep within myself, and the idea of rollerblading for AIDS came to me in a meditation. I was going to rollerblade around the world for AIDS. The rage in me drove me forward. I started the non-profit organization, Blade For AIDS, Inc. This project was going to keep me busy and do my part for humanity. Once again, I was wronged. The event was so successful that AIDS organizations and sponsors started to fight over who was going to be the beneficiary of the event. It was a political mess. A volunteer tried to seize my position as the founder. Again, how could they do this to me? Why is everyone against me? Because of these back-to-back incidents, I no longer had trust in business or in love relationships. I was wronged and then some! I felt I had every right to be angry and not forgive. After all, I was not at fault.

For the next nine years of my life I was stuck, limited, homeless, hungry, and completely fear-based. I was shattered and bankrupt in every area of my life. If only I had forgiven earlier. Every door that I tried to open remained closed. Doors slammed in my face everywhere. My spirit was beaten. Why was this happening to me? The poor me syndrome set in and stayed. All that I had was my sobriety. I learned to rely on God on a daily basis. I pointed the finger always at 'him' or 'them.' I could not forgive because I did nothing wrong (or so I thought). Oh, poor me. I went from a spirited, loving woman to a pain-ridden, penniless and angry woman.

I was to told to pray for that person and the event for thirty days from someone in Alcoholics Anonymous. With no other strengths but fourteen years of sobriety, I did as I was told. It was strongly suggested that I not speak about this person again until I had done the prayer work. I did. I blessed that person and the organization that I resented. I prayed with fervor because I had reached my emotional, financial and spiritual bottom. I prayed that this man and the event receive all the blessing that they desire. This was difficult to do but I did it anyway. This one action is so profound...and it worked! I found it in my heart to forgive after days of continued prayer. The lightness I felt after I fully and completely forgave was miraculous. My resentment was removed. I lost nine miserable years of my life being stubborn, knowing I was right. Since that day miracles have followed miracles in my life. New doors have opened in powerful ways. My physical body has healed. I regained my spirit and then some. All of my dreams have come true!

Today my life is filled with joy, success, creativity, abundance and love, with enough to share with everyone. Consequently, the Blade for AIDS event is still going on successfully under the guise of a different name. The ex lover, wherever you are, I hope you are as happy as I am today.

It took a lot of time to give up on past mistakes and missed opportunities. This forgiving of myself has freed me from my Cinderella victim mentality. So the miracle is to live in the moment each and every day.

Turn within and make a list of people, places and things you need to forgive, and forgive with a true heart. You might need to forgive a situation, a place or an institution. Search out your heart and forgive. Be relentless in your acts of forgiveness.

Jesus himself said that we must forgive our enemies seventy times seven over.

Pause and remember that we are all spirits connected to our individual souls. Each soul has its own growth path and life lessons. Things often happen to us that cause great pain and hardship. And we wonder why. Try to merely forgive even the unforgivable. You are your life changes. When painful lessons come to you embrace and accept them as part of the divine plan.

The event that occurred on September 11, 2001, at the World Trade Center and at the Pentagon, was clearly an unjustifiable act of violent terror resulting in the death of thousands of innocent people. Forgiveness in such circumstances seems almost impossible. However, only through the collective practice of forgiveness of the terrorists can we hope to reclaim peace within ourselves. Forgiveness is the hallmark of love. One can only soften hate with love. Love and forgiveness go hand in hand.

As a student of prosperity, practicing forgiveness can be incorporated into every area of your life. But how?

Missions for Forgiveness

Plan a half-hour of forgiveness work each day.

Commit to memory these two rules:

Bless a thing and it will bless you.

Curse a thing and it will curse you.

The Forgiveness List.

Make a list all persons, places, circumstances, and institutions that you need to forgive. Mentally go through the list and practice this affirmation:

I fully and freely forgive.

I lose and let go.

I forgive everybody and everything.

Say the name of the person or place and state:

*I fully and freely forgive*__________________________

for ____.

Have you ever accused anyone of an unjust grievance? Do you feel you have been wronged in some way? Ask yourself this question: what was my part in the situation that caused the resentment? Was there anything that I could have done to make it better? Was there a lesson to be learned? If the same situation occurs again, what can I do differently?

Observe yourself honestly. This act takes tremendous courage on your part. Bless the grievance and forgive. Bless the situation completely.

I forgive myself... and let go... and let God in.

Each time you silently or aloud send forgiveness to the person, the event, or institution that caused the pain, you are lessoning the charge of that pain. The object is to release you. You are the focus of the forgiveness.

The Watch Mission

Name the person you need to forgive. In the morning when you are getting ready for the day take your watch and put it on the opposite wrist. During the day when you go to look at your watch, you will notice that it is on the wrong wrist. This is your cue to practice forgiveness. Take a breath and silently forgive that person and state the following: Our time together is past and I forgive you. Or Affirm, "I am letting go of past pain. I forgive and let go of yesterday. My time is valuable, I live in happiness. I forgive and let the universe do its perfect work for me."

Snack Attack

We all love our snacks. Pick out your favorite snack: popcorn, M&Ms or peanut butter cups. Attach to the snack food that person or event in need of your urgent forgiveness. Each time you find yourself reaching for the snack food think of the forgiveness you are sending that person. With snack in hand affirm, "I forgive you and release you to your better good. I am at my better place going to my perfect place. I set you free. I am free to enjoy my life." Enjoy your snack, of course, and feel the lightness from the forgiveness.

The Liberating Muse

You have worked the other forgiveness missions and still you are in total bondage from a devastating blow and crippled with resentment. Well, here's some good news: this last mission will liberate you.

For the next thirty days, bless and pray for the persons or places that need it, honestly desiring that they become happy and peaceful. Pray that only the best comes to them. Pray that they receive nothing but blessings in their life, and that all their dreams come true.

Practicing forgiveness daily, removes old negative patterns that are stored in our conscious and subconscious minds. As you forgive yourself and others, divine ideas and new channels and avenues of success, prosperity and abundance will come to you!

Forgiveness is the key
That opens the gateway
Toward removing inequities
Amongst others-
And
Sets upon a new
And profound task
Of awareness
Of truth
And clarity
That soothes
The broken hearted

Notes on Forgiveness

Forgiveness list:

Make a list of all persons, places, institutions and circumstances you need to forgive

I forgive________________for ____________________

I forgive________________for ____________________

Liberating muse

I commit to pray for____________________________

for the next 30 days.

I bless them with a hundred blessings.

The 30-day Mental Fast

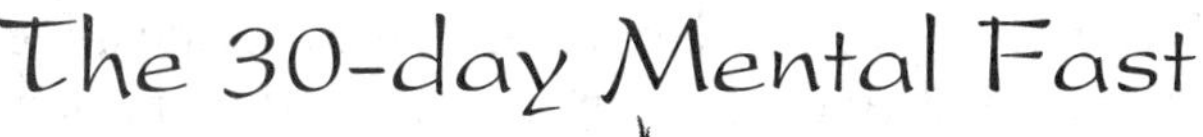

"Faith plus action = success"
Mary Beth Murawski

If you knew that whatever you spoke aloud – or the thoughts in your mind have an eighty-nine percent likelihood of becoming "real" – wouldn't you choose your words more carefully? Our words are the weapons through which we mold our whole life.

The next step to achieving permanent prosperity is to begin the thirty-day *Mental Fast*. This mental mission has been the element in guiding thousands to achieve abundance and prosperity in their lives. The *Mental Fast* is the push-ups of Boot Camp, yet the one that produces immediate results. This mental mission consists of thinking, speaking and acting every minute of every day in a positive manner for thirty consecutive days. Try fasting or refraining from all ill thoughts and negativity.

Our body is a machine that is driven by thought. Your body has memory. Your muscles have memory. Your lungs remember to breathe and your body functions take place even as you sleep. Your mental mechanism goes on and on with conscious and unconscious thoughts. You must speak with authority to your conscious mind to change your memorized negative responses.

When an idea pops into your head, the body responds with an action response. The goal is to manage your thoughts. If you can manage your thoughts, you can master your world. Your mind cannot imagine any solution other than what you tell it. The trick is to retrain your thoughts by consistently declaring thoughts and words of excellence and optimism.

Every thought, word and action must be positive and affirm the good you want your life to be. If you find yourself in a situation that is pessimistic or negative in any way, do not react. Bless the situation, the person, event or feeling and move out of the situation. The most important lesson here is to speak words every day that conform to positive, happy, success induced thoughts.

So far, the missions have been easy. Get ready! Now comes the more difficult part of the prosperity process. To begin the thirty-day *Mental Fast*, first pick your starting date. We recommend not delaying your starting date, as it will only postpone your good or your prosperity from coming to you.

If you find yourself starting to gossip about someone, bless that person to their highest good and reframe from any additional gossip by changing the subject. If gossip is going on around you, simply excuse yourself and gently remove yourself form the situation.

If you are in a traffic jam and feel frustrated, just say aloud, "I love this day," or "God, this is great," and let it go. If for some reason within the thirty days you say words of anger, unhappiness or resentment, simply forgive yourself… cancel the thoughts in the universe and start the *Mental Fast* over again. If you have completed three days or ten days and still have a negative thought or outburst, we strongly suggest that you start all over again, beginning with day one.

At the end of your *Mental Fast*, you will have achieved thirty consecutive days of positive, happy, life affirming thoughts and actions. It is as simple as that. It may take some of you a few months to get the thirty days in a row completed. Don't give up!

The traffic jams were a difficult challenge for me. I would bring a tape in the car to listen away my frustration. It helped. I now have a full library of tapes. Remember, I lived in New York City. Keep the congestion out of your mind and on the road. Be clever. Find a new way to learn something new while driving in traffic.

If you find yourself in lack in any way, it is because your words and your thoughts or a combination have brought you there. As you stop saying phrases like, "I never have any luck...I can't believe how stupid I am...I can't do that," you will hear other people using these negative phrases and your ears will burn with, "I can't believe I used to sound like that!"

When you automatically speak with ease such as, "I am charmed...I am blessed," or "I am inspired today," your attitude will automatically respond. Just try it for yourself and find out.

There is only one way to reach harmony, prosperity, health and peace of mind. As Emmit Fox states in the *Sermon On The Mount*, "that is [done] by bringing about a radical and permanent change for the better in his own consciousness."

As you say the prospering words over and over again… and then over again…you affirm them into existence. You will then find that you will live the life that you have created from your words, thoughts and actions. In other words, if you say, "I am rich, well and happy," then you will be. If you say, "I am sick and tired," you will be. Your body will obey and respond to whatever you tell it.

During your thirty day *Mental Fast*, it is strongly suggested that you remove the following thoughts or words from your vocabulary:

sarcasm	negative thoughts
fear and resentment	all forms of gossip
all forms of criticism	

If at any moment you find yourself thinking negatively, you must start your thirty-day *Mental Fast* all over again. You will discover once you break the negative patterns from your subconscious mind (and this will take time), you will begin to experience a new attitude and outlook toward life. People will become attracted to you. Events and circumstances will come to you effortlessly. You will be well on your way to receiving all the good that you desire. If you have an interesting story that has a "life changing effect," please feel free to email us at any time. We know and appreciate the value of a true success story, and would love to hear your progress in success and prosperity!

Drive the thoughts of anger, loss and depression right out of your consciousness. They are intruders and have no business being there. They are trying to rob you of peace, contentment and joy. Evict them today! Stay focused on speaking righteous thoughts and words. When fear, frustration and anger attempt to take hold of you, stay calm and centered on the peace within. Continue to do this until you are completely at ease. Walk away from anger or any negative emotion. Watch your emotions and thoughts like a guard dog. Speak and think only positive, happy thoughts. Above all, speak the truth. In order to manifest your new belief system or desire, speak and affirm them aloud. Speaking your goals, dreams and wishes out loud in affirmation form is very powerful. This shatters and breaks up the old pattern to allow for the new dream (desire) to take form. This takes time and a whole lot of patience. But in the end you will see that your efforts have been well worth it.

Thinking habits are the most subtle yet one of the most powerful to break. Do not invest your emotions toward anger, doubt, fear, jealously or resentment. These emotions deplete your energy. And what do you gain from them? Nothing. But you can lose quite a lot. Negative emotions rob you of your power, your strength, your creativity and passion. When you change your thoughts and change your words, you change your life! If a negative thought such as anger appears, just stop. Remain still, and take three deep breaths. Change the pattern verbally by affirming a positive approach. Simply affirm your new thought into existence. This means, to speak out loud your new intentions, thoughts or feelings. It will take time to cancel out the negative patterns, but once the new belief system is in place, the miracle will transpire within you.

If you follow the thirty-day fast, we guarantee you will be well on your way to living life prosperously, abundantly and with joy!

Here are some tools to help you keep on your *Mental Fast* mission.

1. Every day, tie a string around your wrist to help you remember to speak only with the purest of thought. The string will remind you to stay focused on positive responses only.

2. Playing the opposite of the negative emotion.

Play this game when harmful emotions are tempting your *Mental Fast*. Play the opposite whenever destructive emotions appear.

When you feel frustration coming up in a situation, just laugh. Play the opposite of the emotion. Say aloud, "Wow, this is really funny." Or, "God, can you see how funny this is." Just start laughing when you feel frustrated.

What do you do with anger? When Anger comes up, applaud, clap your hands and cheer...yell "Bravo!" The opposite of an anger response is the explosion of fun. Jump up and down if you have to. Try a physical action...take a walk, do some push ups, breathe in slowly. Use the anger to create a different response, thus playing the opposite emotion. Don't hold in the anger only to explode later.

What do you do when fear or confusion engulfs every part of your being? Confusion and fear can paralyze you.

Affirm: *All fear is false. Fear is not fact.*

Taking a physical action always removes mental clutter. Run, jog or go to the gym. Get a full glass of water. Stand over the sink and pour it down the drain. As you are pouring the water, focus on the fearful thoughts empting from your mind. Clear your mind and be one with God. Fear will stop us from moving forward. Confusion will create chaos.

FEAR Forget Everything And Run.

Have you ever spent the whole day staying stuck in your own drama by analyzing a situation or problem to death? It never serves us to go over and over in our thoughts why things go wrong. The circumstances or difficulties that caused the problem will never be changed through obsessive analyzing. Get yourself unstuck by moving your body and doing something that you are familiar with.

Make yourself a sandwich or pop some popcorn. Watch an old video of your favorite TV show. Go to the movies or take a walk in a familiar place. Take a ride in the car and blast some fun music. No sad songs please.

When you move your body it lessens the charge of the emotion. Take on a physical action that grounds you. Stop thinking or over-thinking the situation. Take a time out with yourself, and focus on the direct opposite action. Sit down and have a cup of tea.

We are not suggesting you avoid your responsibilities by playing the opposite. But we want to make it as clear as possible that operating out of fear, anger and confusion will not produce harmony in your life. When you play the opposite game, it keeps people interested and wondering what you are up to as you handle everything so gracefully.

Continue daily in your reprieve against speaking and thinking ill thoughts. Do this untiringly until all your thoughts and words are positive, to flood across the stage of consciousness in pure uninterrupted wavelengths. Soon your automatic response will be that of positive words and constructive thinking. Like radio waves that transmit through the ethers, your words and thoughts will do the same. They will send out 'the good' that you want to receive.

Please email us to let us know the benefits or your *Mental Fast*. You will be amazed at what good you will attract in your life just by doing this *Mental Fast* diet.

Mental Fast Check Point

I am committed to start my *Mental Fast* on:

Day ____________________

Month _________________

Year ___________________

Keep a record of your negative thoughts, words and actions. Write down when anger comes up for you. Write down when negative thoughts and reactions occur throughout the day. What can I do differently, so that I will not respond negatively in the future?

____

____

____

____

____

____

____

____

____

____

Doodle Space

We have a chat room on our website where you can share your support, questions and successes.

Flash Cards and Pin-Ups

The law of the universe states: Whatever you constantly look at and 'see' becomes the subject of your reality.

Do you remember flash cards as a learning tool when you were a child? They had pictures on them to identify ducks, cows and pigs. Our flash cards are similar. They are the visual tools that you will constantly look at reminding your subconscious mind of your desires, wants and needs. You will gather together pictures, images and icons of what you want from your Master Plan. Place these pictures and icons on large index cards or in a notebook. You also can make a large poster card and hang it on your wall. The flash cards are a simple yet effective visual tool that sends a message to your subconscious or higher self. Learn the value of simplicity. You may be surprised when you discover how much teaching power there can be in very simple things.

It is difficult to accomplish anything if you cannot see yourself or truly believe that you can accomplish and receive whatever you desire. Your success and happiness is largely dependent on your ability to visualize and see your success already at hand. You will remain poised and balanced when the goal is attained because you have visualized the outcome.

Daily you will look at your flash cards or flip through your flash book. This step of looking at your flash card is another important tool for the imaging process. Your subconscious mind needs constant visual re-enforcement in order to manifest your desires. Remember, whatever you constantly look at and *see* becomes the subject of your reality.

When the desires manifest and become yours, write notes on the back of your cards to remind you of what events and circumstances brought you to your success. Try to keep track of how the universe works for you and how your goals are realized through divine winning.

Keep your flash cards that have already manifested. On a day when you are losing faith, take out the card and read how the circumstances brought you to obtaining this desire. As you read, feel the joy of faith re-surge within you.

Here is your mission: Go back to your Master Plan and or what you wrote down in phase one. Choose from your *I want list* several desires. Then look through magazines for photos or find photographs of exactly what you want. Cut out the photos or icons and paste them on cards or in a notebook. The photographs that you choose must be pictures of what you listed in your Master Plan, or what you wrote down. Carefully choose pictures of exactly what you want.

You can also use phrases and words. If you find a phrase from a newspaper or magazine that motivates you, cut it out and put it on a flash card. We call these cards 'pin ups', which are really great for spot check viewing in times of doubt. Try typing out an affirmation and print it out in bold letters. Or, write an affirmation on a card with a bright magic marker. As you glance at your pin-ups throughout the day, it strengthens your visual imaging process. As you look at your pin-ups, soon the words will become your physical reality.

Two years ago, I put together a poster pin-up. In big, black, bold numbers I wrote out $35,000.00 dollars. I needed this amount to buy my dream home. I wrote this statement out in full faith that I would receive it. I believed that the money would come to me in God's own wonderful way. In addition, I asked that the funds be delivered within ninety days. I placed daisies all around the poster that I put over my bed. I looked at it every evening with excitement and great anticipation. The following events happened within a few weeks.

I was asked to administer a training school in New York City one week after I made my flash card. That week an ad was placed in the *New York Times* Sunday issue and the phone rang off the hook for students. $35,000 dollars was delivered to me in less than two months. I received the right and perfect amount of money for my dream home! This all happened because I had faith that it would and I expected that my good would come!

Place your flash card photos or pin-up phrases around your home, office or dorm room. For example: place this pin-up phrase outside your shower, *I am getting stronger and stronger each and every day.* Next to your mirror, place the icon of the new computer that you need. Over the visor of your car, place the photo of your new car, blessing your old car for its service. For that well deserved vacation, cut out a picture from a travel magazine of a beautiful tropical island. Place this next to the tub. View the photo as you soak into your holiday retreat.

Pin-up a photo next to your morning mirror, your briefcase, knapsack, coffee pot and, of course, the obvious refrigerator. Do you want a new pair of rollerblades? Then go to a sports shop and get a photo of the rollerblades you would love to own. Do you want to receive your dream home? Then buy a key chain for the new house. Make up a graduation certificate of the college you want to attend, or a clean bill of health to hang on your wall. Do you want happiness and joy in your life? Then find a happy and healthy picture of yourself and pin it up. Do you want the right and perfect job? You could draft a signed mock contract of a new job offer with the right salary that you declare. You can get very creative here. I heard of an Olympic athlete who carried around in his pocket a magazine photo of a gold medal. Wherever you can, place a visual image of your desire and view it often.

Take your pictures (either photographs or from the magazines) and phrases and pin-up words that you have carefully chosen and view them throughout the day. It is most important that you saturate your subconscious mind with your desires. Whatever images and thoughts you send to your higher self will be the demonstration of the *good* you receive.

Visualize and feel the pictures, phrases and words as becoming your reality. Feel it, know it, accept it and believe it. You must *feel* the pictures, as though you are already in the picture and *be* in the vibration of the pictures that you radiate. To establish vision means to *see clearly* and feel you are living inside of the pictures. Make it as real as possible. All people who have accomplished great things have done this! Visualize and feel the pictures, phrases and words as becoming an authentic part of your life. Did you ever wonder why successful people who are ahead of their time (such as Michelangelo or Leonardo DeVinci), are called *visionaries*? Because they were able to visualize things that others weren't even thinking about. They never let limitations stand in the way of the creative process. Learn from the examples of the great men and women of history. There is no doubt that they understood exactly what we are talking about here. They knew how to visualize and then embrace positive things, and in turn made them a very real part of their extraordinary lives.

When you have completed your flash cards and pin-up phrases remember to hold the mental pictures of yourself succeeding. Your conscious mind will seek to transcend those images to you. Hold the pictures in your mind tenaciously. Do not let the image fade or become unclear. And most of all do not doubt the reality of the images that you have created. Practice believing in full faith that you will receive. Continue to hold the picturization firmly in your thoughts. You will be astonished at the wonderful ways in which the picture comes to pass.

Your pictures and pin-up phrases must be exactly what you want to manifest in your life. Pay attention to the details of the words and pictures. Make sure that whatever you place on your cards is really what you want.

A unity student in New York City placed a picture of a man that she desired for her relationship on her card. She just loved the look of the man from the magazine. Months later, she was in a relationship with a man who looked similar to the man on her card. He ended up having a drinking problem. Later she went back to review her photo. With a closer look, she noticed the man was holding a can of beer in his hands. Hence, be very clear when choosing your pictures, words and photographs.

Notes on *Flash Cards and Pin-Ups*

Doodle Space

Kahuna Prayer

"Faith is a combination of simple requests or little prayers being answered."

Mary Beth Murawski

Huna may be called a philosophy or an esoteric study of miracles. Some consider *Huna* to be a religion because it has "religious" concepts such as prayer-action. In this chapter, we will give you a brief introduction to the powerful *Kahuna* prayer.

Huna™ is the name given by Max Freedom Long to the system he discovered and synthesized over fifty years off research. *Huna*, then, is a practical system of psychology and magical prayer Mr. Long used by the *Kahuna* priests of ancient Hawaii. The *Kahuna* priests kept the *Kahuna* prayer as their closely guarded secret for centuries.

Max Freedom Long chose the word *Huna* in the 1930s to describe the religious/psychological methods used by the *Kahuna* priest. *Huna* is the Hawaiian word for secret. The *Kahuna*'s were "the keepers of the secret" in performing their particular kinds of miracles. The magical *Kahuna* prayer is part of the Huna philosophy. *Huna* is about healing the spirit, mind, and body. Through this healing system, you will become one with yourself and the universe.

The *Kahuna* prayer is a ritual performed by the ancient *Kahuna* priest from Hawaii. This ancient practice of performing miracles has been with the Hawaiian priest for many centuries. It is a powerful tool that miraculously answers prayers. The *Kahuna* prayer considers the powers of the mind to be natural and inherent in everyone. The *Kahuna* prayer teaches that everyone is directly connected to God. The secret of this healing and prosperity method is that you are securing the express ability to contact your higher self or subconscious self. It is based on the knowledge of how the three levels of consciousness or the *three selves* function effectively when working harmoniously together to receive your prayer request.

The *Ha* or *Kahuna* prayer is a mere guideline, an introduction to the *Ha* ritual prayer. By following the steps to the miraculous *Kahuna* prayer, you can obtain the key to unlocking a simple yet proven way to have your prayers answered. It is also important for you to note that we do not promise or guarantee that you will become a *Kahuna* master by practicing this prosperity method. Nor do we claim to be *Kahuna* or *Huna* masters ourselves. We are simply introducing the concept to you.

Max Freedom Long studied the *Kahuna* masters of Hawaii for almost forty years. He sums up the *Kahuna* prayer in the following manner. "Construct a picture of yourself in perfect health with manna the vital force. Manna according to the *Kahuna* is the vital force within each of us to create. This will permit a lasting thought-form picture to be sent to the high self or subconscious mind. In order to create the manna or vital force you must breathe."

In order to perform the *Kahuna* prayer properly you will need to understand manna as well as the three aspects of self. Manna is the vital creative force that energizes and heals. Manna is constructed or formed by breathing in deep clear breaths. Manna *is* your breath.

The *Kahuna* prayer deals with three aspects of self. The lower self (*unihipili*), the middle self (*uhane*), or your conscious self, and your higher self (the *aumakua*). The lower self and the middle self are under the guidance and protection of the *aumakua*, the higher self. The *aumakua* occupies the level of consciousness immediately above our own conscious level or our all powerful higher selves. The goal in the *Kahuna* prayer is to send our desires from our lower self and middle self up to our subconscious self. In order to have the *Kahuna* prayer work, all three parts of self must be in complete agreement with each other. When this shift occurs, your prayer is answered!

The powerful *Kahuna* prayer connects all three parts of our self to one. Another objective in the *Kahuna* prayer is to increase your manna, or the vital creative force that is within you. We all have manna that is within us. Manna is our breath of life. The *Kahuna* prayer works by sending manna (your breath...your creative force, your pure intentions...thoughts, dreams and goals made from your list) from your conscious self to your higher self. Your higher self or your *aumakua* has an incredible amount of power.

The most essential way to achieve success or have your prayers answered is to contact your higher self or superconscious self. This is done by connecting all aspects of self to be in agreement with each other. The message (visual image from your flash cards) is sent to the higher self through pure intention manna or breaths. This action must be consistent and repetitive. As you continue to practice daily, your prayer is manifested. Your higher self is capable of anything.

The *Ha* prayer or *Kahuna* ritual must be constant and repetitive. In order to receive maximum results you must send the same picture continually. Take your visual images from your flash cards and send those images followed by breath to your higher self. Do not change your images, as this will only delay your good. Be clear and concise. The *Kahuna* prayer must be repeated over and over again until your good or what you visualize is realized. We recommend doing the *Kahuna* prayer in the morning ten times and in the evening before you go to bed. The easiest way to put your dream forward is to increase the manna or vital force that naturally flows through you. This is done with breath.

To begin the *Kahuna* prayer

Refer to your master list that you wrote down and your flash cards that you created.

Clear your mind into nothingness by breathing ten deep breaths.

Form a clear picture in your mind of your desired goals.

Take four deep breaths each time sending a clear and conscious visual picture of what you want. At the same time look at your flash cards, and use those images to send to your sub conscious through your breath. Stay focused.

Remove all fear and guilt from your thoughts and actions.

Repeat this prayer by taking once again four deep clear breaths. Then send the mental picture from your flash cards and what you wrote down up to your higher self.

As soon as you feel the images…thoughts...and pictures as becoming part of your reality, your prayer will be answered.

Remember...

Try not to harm others.

Always attach faith to your Kahuna *prayer.*

Everything starts with breath.

Breath is the only connection to the soul.

This prayer will not fail!

Notes on *Kahuna Prayer*

The *Kahuna* prayer is the combination of all imaging missions in alignment with the three aspects of self.

Have I removed fear and guilt from my thoughts and actions before I perform the *Kahuna* Prayer?

The clear picture in my mind is: (describe)

Repeat the *Kahuna* prayer at least once a day and continue until your answer is given. And have faith!

Doodle Space

Giving & Receiving

"Faith is knowing that you always have something to give."

Mary Beth Murawski

Give what you want to receive. You cannot receive without giving. The giver and the receiver are the same. It is the continual tidal flow of the giving and receiving that is the prerequisite to prosperity. As you become familiar with the process of giving that which you desire to receive, the abundance of the universe is made possible in our lives. By giving to others exactly what you desire you are sealing your own good to come forth.

We all have wealth and success permanently inherent in our all-knowing mind. Today, you are asked to tap into that source. The answer is through giving. This opens the well of prosperity toward the fulfillment of your dreams.

I once met a very wise woman while living in Los Angeles in the mid 90s. She was very successful in every area of her life. Her presence was one of poise, and a silent confidence surrounded her being. She was charming, funny and all-knowing. I was going through yet another challenging period in my life. I had nothing but my sobriety and was barely holding on to that. My spirit was beginning to disconnect from my body. I was confused and had little ability to even concentrate on anything positive or uplifting. I was stuck and felt miserable. Nothing was working in my life. My funds were limited, living hand to mouth, all the while being in full-blown fear. If only I knew at the time to change my thoughts, my words, my actions and my attitude. This woman told me, "Mary Beth, give what you don't have! When you apply this truth for yourself, you will attain whatever it is that your heart desires."

I thought about those words of wisdom for many years. "Give what you do not have." Did this mean I had to go and get what I did not have and give it away in order to really receive? On the other hand, did it mean I should 'give up' everything no matter what it was in order to receive my greater good? It took many years of contemplation and solid "alone time" to come up with the right answer for me. Several years later, I found myself yet again in the same situation. I continued to recreate the same patterns over and over in my life. This time, it was in New York City. The pattern of lack, limitation, and depression, was an extremely hard condition to overcome. Every day was filled with hopelessness from which I could not seem to break out to find the truth. Yet I know now that my higher self was repeating the same lesson until I really understood all the various forms of lack and limitation and the dangers of my many negative thinking patterns.

While in New York City, I was living day to day in faith that my life would change for the better. I once again surrendered to God...that He would take care of me. I had created many vacuum periods in my life. I gave away furniture, jewelry and my car, while leaving Los Angeles. The only thing I had of value was my healing crystal.

This crystal was my rock and my strength during years of trying times. This quartz crystal gave me hope and a sense of strength. I carried it with me in the right pocket of my pants.

While in a complete daze one afternoon, I was walking in the Chelsea district of New York City. I saw a young man walking. He was carrying a backpack that was overloaded. He looked tired. He had a wooden leg and was trying to attach it to his limb. My heart went out to him. I knew that this was the time.

This was the person. I had to give my healing crystal to this stranger. The man looked at me oddly, as I explained why I was giving him this gift. He took the crystal and was grateful for my kindness. I had given something that I did not have – understanding.

The law of truth in understanding is that as you begin to acquire understanding in your life it is then that the outer picture of your life immediately improves. This change in "what you get" or the outer picture is the visible evidence of the change inside of your consciousness.

I gave understanding and the acknowledgement of another human being for his strength. The power of understanding and true compassion from the deepest part of me freed my spirit. The law of understanding is as follows: that as you acquire an inner knowing of understanding, then the outer picture of your life immediately improves. This change in your world is the visible evidence of the change inside of consciousness or mind. As I gave what I did not have, I began to receive kindness from strangers. Honest and straightforward individuals who could understand my situation with compassion and understanding came forward pointing me in desirable directions. I got it. Give what you do not have, or give what you want to receive and you will receive it. This experience also prepared me to have the ability to receive. This was another lesson testing me to find the truth. I am a very proud woman, and receiving was hard to accept. I used to question why people wanted to give, thinking, "What is the motive behind this?" This new freedom was a turning point for my prosperity. I learned that giving can be a humbling experience.

Mission

Find an object that was given to you and is sentimental, yet of no great value to anyone else but you. Place this on your dresser or nightstand This is your reminder of giving to others.

For ten days, give something to someone

Buy cards that express love or gratitude

Give of your time to listen to someone who needs help. You will be heard

Give a pat on the back to someone in need

Make lunch for a friend

Visit an old age home

Volunteer at an event

Give someone flowers

Make a card and send it

It is through spiritual growth that these blessings are promised to come.

Second, give to yourself. It is possible to give too much to others and not enough to yourself. Attend to the nurturing parts of your self. Over giving to others can deplete you of energy and further bring about lack into your life. Start by doing something special for yourself. It might be as simple as taking an hour-long bath. Purchasing a book or meditation tape. Take yourself out on a date and do something you have always wanted to do. Give yourself quiet time to go within. Being kind to yourself daily enables the flow of kindness that can come from you.

Mission

Below is a list of focused acts of kindness for you. Add to this list your own fun idea. Put all the ideas on scrap paper. Fold them up and put them in a bowl. Pick one a day and do it.

Take a walk in nature

Call an old friend just to say hello

Organize a chapter of "The Too Much Fun Club" with friends, and meet weekly just to have fun

Plan a dream vacation

Take a healing essential oil bath

Read a joke book and laugh with yourself

Draw your wishes in the sand at the beach

Put make-up on or take make-up off

In the middle of the day, change your socks (it feels great)

Take time to pray

Rent or buy a scooter and have fun

Go and pick wild flowers for your night table or purchase flowers for yourself

Go shopping and get one item you want that is not on sale.

Buy a teddy bear and put a bandana around it marked with "I am prosperous now"

Decorate your house in vibrant colors

Hug yourself gently

Tie a bath towel around your neck like a cape and be your own action hero. Captain Cape!

Tithing

The Oxford Dictionary says Tithe: is one tenth of annual product of land or labor.

The law of increase and tithing has been around since Moses and Abraham. The magical number of increase is ten. The ancient prophets believed in giving ten percent of all of their income. They always prospered when they gave ten percent of their crops or earned income to their place of worship. When they did not tithe ten percent of their income, everything seemed to go wrong.

Giving ten percent back to God sealed their prosperity and made it permanent. Many of the ancient tribes in Biblical times also believed that tithing protected them from disease, famine and drought.

Tithing may seem at first to be very difficult. But this form of giving sets in motion an unparalleled security that always fosters and brings about prosperity. It is divine law and it states:

> *Tithe money to your church, or the religious organization or source from which you receive spiritual strength.*

First, give back to God and tithe. As you give, so shall you receive. It is through spiritual growth that these blessings are promised to come to you. If your economic outlook is bleak, tithing will open the way to success and prosperity.

Everyone has something to give. If your bank account is zero then give of your time, talent and energy. Just watch how the law of tithing will move you forward to your greater good. If you are on financial assistance, you may feel this is impossible. Nothing is impossible. You can start to tithe ten percent of your time and talent right now. Tithe what you can of the money you receive. Your finances will grow and you will soon be able to tithe the ten percent. If you are financially well off, still tithe ten percent of your time, talent and financial income. True prosperity will happen to you as you begin to tithe your way to riches. Remember, this is a rich and friendly universe. As you give ten percent of your income to God, so will your income increase.

If we do not give to God, to ourselves or to others, then our life becomes unbalanced or unequal. When you withhold from the universe you may experience some form of withholding in your life. It might be lack of supply in your life, lack of health, lack of love, or lack of direction. Nevertheless, you will undergo unnecessary *dis-ease*.

On a closing note, having the ability to receive gracefully is an art form within itself. When you are given an unexpected compliment or kindness, how do you respond?

How do you feel? Do you shift your body posture or shuffle your feet? Learn to receive from others gracefully. Not with, "ah shucks it was nothing." Giving is a powerful way to open the flow of prosperity. You must not diminish your acts of kindness.

Start by giving ten percent of your income. Give of your time talent and energy. Give of your time by volunteering. To your church, to your temple, your mosque or to the group you attend, and from whom you receive your spiritual food. Give of your talents, your energy and your resources. Give freely, joyfully without attachment.

As we conclude this section on giving and receiving, please note that *Secrets of Prosperity* is not a "get rich quick scheme" (although some will manifest money quickly). Rather, it is an enriching daily program that unlocks the truth to your everyday prosperity. This is a daily agenda of how to build on self-love and bring to a close the uncertainties brought on with constant worry. Let go, and let a Higher Power remove the long-standing negative patterns that rule your life. The first way to change the world is to empower yourself.

Below are affirmations on giving and receiving and tithing:

As I give freely, unconditionally, and with no attachments, I thereby am enabled to receive in even greater measure.

As I give of my time of my talents and of my income, I receive divine blessings abundantly.

My desires are my blessings waiting for me to receive them.

My Father in heaven gives with pleasure and I gladly receive with thanksgiving and joy!

I am worthy of receiving all the good God has for me now. I accept and claim my abundant good this day. My good is here now.

I am no longer blocked by lack of giving. If I am in lack or limitations in any area of my life, I choose to give more. Through my sincere act of giving, I remove all blocks and I receive joyously!

I give up all false ideas of receiving. I am a child of God; therefore, I am willing to receive.

I am receiving now. I am receiving all the wealth that exists in the universe now.

I receive permanent prosperity now. I live in a loving and abundant universe.

Divine love gives me all that I desire in my heart now.

I receive my demonstration freely, quickly, and without reservation now. I receive my good quickly, effortlessly, and without reservation now.

I give thanks that I have received all that I desire under God's divine timing.

God is the source of my good. Therefore, I give praise and thanksgiving to God now.

I am a blessed child of God, and God wants only the best for me now.

I gladly and joyously receive my dreams today. Thank-you God, for my good.

I am a deserving child of God and I receive my divine blessings with a welcoming and deserving heart.

God's blessings can operate in my finances since God is the source of our supply.

If you want more leisure time in your life, then give freely and unconditionally of your time.

If you want more love in your life then give more love to others.

As you bless and release your money, this keeps the flow of money coming back to you by growing and flowing.

Notes on Giving, Receiving and Tithing

Doodle Space

Chapter 9 Convergence

Faith already knows...that all is well, no matter what happens or what the outcome is.

Mary Beth Murawski

Converge...to come to, or toward, the same point. The convergence is where the negative and positive meet, it 'shakes us up.' Our negative thoughts or negative patterns that have held back our happy successful living, now manifest in physical ways, and the old habits may appear to win at first. This shake-up period can appear to be failure when in fact the opposite is true. Your initial reaction will be to retreat to the former, more familiar and safer patterns of behavior. It is common to experience a lot of stress during this period. The seeming blocks or problems that you experience are actually the new positive thoughts being brought to the surface of the situation. You can even rejoice in your cleansing process. This can also be interpreted as a test or a lesson in prosperity. For example, when applying medicine to a wound, the stinging means that healing is taking place.

This cleansing period causes a polarity shift. You are tapping into the subconscious mind where old patterns of negative thought are hiding. You are replacing the negative with optimistic thoughts, affirmations and positive behavior. This clash of positive and negative is like two magnets that are reversed, trying to push each other apart.

The convergence is a competition of the wills between the long forgotten negative behaviors and the newborn positive programming. A mental duel will take place inside your unconscious mind. As this happens, you will encounter a variety of experiences. This will cause a temporary delay on the road to your greater good. The old saying, "things usually get worse before they get better" can easily apply here. But don't be scared or intimidated. This is all natural. And you will indeed overcome this "choppy seas" portion of your journey and win in the end.

Here is an example of the cleansing process in action. You have prayed for financial independence and suddenly unexpected costs set your bank account on empty. The vacuum law of prosperity can apply here. The expenditures going out of your account are merely creating an opening for your expanded good to come to you. Here's another example: you wrote down that you want perfect health. And you come down with a cold. If you have been ill, then your disease or imbalance might flare up and get even worse. Perhaps you prayed for better relationships with family and friends, and for no apparent reason everyone appears to be against you. You feel inharmonious and in conflict with those around you. Just don't be afraid of these changes. It will certainty pass. During this period of change, try as best as you can to remain calm and be still with yourself.

Take walks... go to the movies... take a healing bath with an essential oil and light some candles... go and visit a sick person (this act works miracles) or clean out an old closet. The point is to be as gentle with yourself as you can. Above all, do not stop working the *Secrets of Prosperity* Program. Have faith and practice living your life as though you have already received the demonstration of your good in advance.

It is at this point in the study of truth and prosperity that many want to quit. People who experience this cleansing process or breakdown of events around them have lived in negative thought for the majority of their lives. You may feel fearful or nervous and slightly agitated while doing your prosperity treatment. It is critical to NOT give up at this point. Remember, others have gone before you. Things will turn out OK. Just don't give up on yourself now. Think how far you have come already!

I call this mental conflict the *innate dualism.* The innate dualism within each of us is a choice of right or wrong, good or bad, negative or positive. They come together making this polarity in thought occur. Eventually the positive or new way of thinking will win out and cancel out the negative. This is your initiation to prosperity. Just know that. This cleansing period takes a lot faith and perseverance. Hold onto patience. Your old way of thinking and speaking will be removed and your good will appear. Something far better will always take its place. There was a lot of wisdom in that old saying, "good things come to those who wait." Live every day in expectation of what is right and good. Affirm the following:

> *I am not afraid. There is no evil in this situation. I accept and embrace this experience now. I am made whole, new and complete again. I am relaxed and have faith that my good is here right now. All is well in my world.*

Meet your cleansing process with acceptance. It will be much easier for you. Try not to fight what is happening to you. Surrender to it.

Emmit Fox calls this process, "chemicalization" and he states: "Chemicalization means that your life is changing, shifting, cleansing and being restored. No matter what is going on in your life, have faith that your good, your demonstration, is right around the corner."

To recap this challenging step: The convergence process delays our good in order to make all things new. It is a deep and thorough cleansing period. It removes lack, limitation, fear, and doubt. It cleanses and restores our mind. It cleanses and restores our emotions. It heals our bodies and our spirits to open the way for the good to come to us. This deep purification process is probably the most difficult phase of *Secrets of Prosperity*. The initiation process can bring the adverse results of your intentions or desires for a brief period of time. It shakes us up and removes negative thoughts and negative belief systems. It gets us unstuck before our good or our dreams are realized.

Remember to hold to your commitment to the *Secrets of Prosperity* while going through the cleansing process. Continue to write down what you want daily. Focus on your goals. Do your affirmations out loud more frequently. View your flash cards as often as you can. Forgive and continue to forgive. Make a love offering to someone in need. Give of yourself if you have no available funds. And most of all, be still. Go to that quiet place within, and know that all is well. The initiation process is a great faith exercise that will help you attain your good.

Occasionally give yourself a consciousness boost by affirming something like:

> *Only good can come from this convergence process. My mind, my emotions and my body are being restored now. I am ready to receive my good. I am permanently prospered now.*

The cleansing process is a clear and inevitable sign that things are getting better. The alteration (sometimes volatile) occurs when an old idea or negative pattern tries to stay with you. At the same time, a new and profound idea or thought is trying to make its entrance into your conscious mind. This understanding will make the experience of the convergence period easier for you.

This process usually occurs before the good is manifested in your life. If your cleansing period is long and challenging then your good is going to be even greater.

The Abundance Mission

For ten days in a row write five different ways in which you see abundance around you.

Abundance is everywhere.

I see abundance in the beautiful green grass.

I see abundance in and through my home.

I see abundance in my bank account.

Create new abundant thoughts each and every day for ten days in a row. This mission will appease your convergence period toward a radical shift in consciousness. There are only four possible attitudes to take in any given situation.

You can believe that things are going to work out and with faith, you see that they do.

You can believe that things are going to work out yet you work hard to see that they do.

You can believe that things are not going to work out, nevertheless you work hard to see that they do.

You believe that things are not going work out and you resign yourself to defeat.

What attitude will you choose during your convergence period? We are going to repeat the cleansing steps because it is at this stage where truth students have a tendency to stop the flow of success.

Steps to Convergence

First: Your old way of thinking is being saturated with the new. The first action is to be gentle with yourself, remain calm and be still. Know that everything eventually passes. Nothing ever stays the same.

Second: Situations and things begin to break-up. You may feel depressed, confused and indecisive during this time. You might even feel out of control. This is all good. Just be still and try to bless the process even though it may be difficult to do. It is imperative not to fight or resist the changes that you are going through. What we resist usually persists.

Third: Rest in faith that all is moving forward in your life for your own greater good. Be one with God. Be still and listen. Although this may be a time of loss and apparent failure, it is only temporary. Meet your challenges calmly and expect to receive your good. Remember that you are growing during this time. Anything that brings about growth in your soul is a success.

Fourth: During the convergence period, you might feel weak. This feeling of weakness in your soul may be the loss of an old personality trait. If someone or something has been removed in your life, it may bring up feelings of loss and sadness. Bless the situation or person and let it go. Let go of all fear. Let go of loss. Do not try to fix anything or manipulate the changes in your life. Welcome the changes with grace.

Fifth: Your good comes after the resting period! Try organizing a weekend with old friends to laugh and just *be*. Rest your mind and do some fun activities. The goal here is to just have fun.

Try living inside of:

Divine fulfillment is now manifested in my life. All is well. Divine fulfillment and prosperity is here.

Faith is understanding that somewhere, somehow there is a reason...a really good reason for our plans to go astray.

Notes on *Convergence*

Look at your convergence period as simply sliding down the other end of the rainbow. Like a rollercoaster, it feels somewhat dangerous and frightening, but isn't there some excitement also? Describe what it feels like to be sliding down the rainbow…can you see the pot of gold at the end?

Doodle Space

Over The Rainbow

Faith in action reminds us that we are never-ending spirits passing through this life to love, to learn and to grow.

Mary Beth Murawski

When you receive your *good*, we call it getting over the rainbow. The phases of *Secrets of Prosperity* have brought you to the brink of a new and profound way of life. New avenues of mental and verbal expression that flood our consciousness have created the physical expression of our desires through the powers of the spirit and God. Upon receiving your demonstration or your *good*, you will expand upward into spiritual consciousness as your dreams and goals excel the boundaries of human imagination and belief spiraling upward toward heaven. Now that you have found this spiritual consciousness from your secret place inside of you, will have perfect vital health, abundant prosperity, and total and complete happiness. Your health will be so wonderful that life will be a mere expression of incomprehensible joy. Your body will be light with winged shoes, like that of an angel. You will feel and live such abundance that money will be supplied to you always and your burdens will be lifted forever. You have reached your pot of gold over the rainbow!

It is not by chance or luck that you have been delivered all that you have now. The demonstration of your good appears in many ways. You will begin to notice that moments you once thought of as chance meetings or events will start to line up correctly and bring you your desired thoughts and images.

You might ask yourself, how do I stay over the rainbow? Now that you are living an abundant life, keep your words and actions pure. Retain the pictures that you continually send to your conscious mind. Guard against negative thinking. Live in forgiveness. Preserve your alone time for prayer and affirmations. Remain true to your daily missions. Keep on creating vacuums and more vacuums. Your new mental livelihood will not fade to the background when you hold to truth in faith.

Changing your consciousness has been no easy task. You have featured yourself in your own mental movie of exactly what you wanted. Now that mental dress rehearsal will play out for real. How did you react? How did you respond when your writing from the heart came true? Did you expect it to happen? Were you surprised yet not surprised? Did you gently smile and say wow, thank you, God?

Affirm the following...this will help renew your mind:

I accept my good with grace and thanksgiving.

As you called upon the universal substance or divine intelligence to prosper you every day, acknowledge it knowing that your good was always there waiting for you to claim it. It is your divine heritage to be happy, peaceful and content.

> *My mind, my body and financial affairs are now filled with the rich universal substance of perfect health, unlimited wealth, success and unconditional love.*

Everything that you wrote down in phase one of *Secrets of Prosperity* will come forth as your demonstration. It is without doubt that your dream or wish will manifest into reality for you. It is only a matter of time. God's time. Be ready for your good to come forth, and wait upon your blessings like a child on the eve of Christmas, because it can flow to you quickly and through miraculous channels. When you accept your new place in life, continue in your prosperity regime with unceasing watchfulness. Stay in the courage. Stay forever open to your blessings. Express your own truth and then live it. Move forward in faith that your needs will always be provided for.

When your good is delivered to you, it means that you have received *substance* from your creator. Your desires, needs, dreams and wishes of what you wrote down become consciousness because you successfully followed your inner spirit. Give praise and thanksgiving to God who has blessed you with infinite supply. In fact, God's supply of substance or *good* never ever runs dry and is always available to you at any moment in time.

You do not have to wait for your good or your expressions of requests to come forth. With unyielding faith, your good is already here. As you continue to receive blessings in your life, continue to bless the blessings and more substance and good will flow to you. You will never again be impoverished if you look to God for your immediate supply. As you accept the bounty of your fruit, you will be crowned with unlimited prosperity. Your well will never ever run empty.

You can also secure your good, or your realization, by making a special prayer of thanksgiving. Whatever you have been blessed with, whether it is a physical healing, the right and perfect partner, or you have achieved financial wealth or financial independence, give praise and thanksgiving to the one and only source of your good — God. Remember, with financial wealth, we give back ten percent to God. Your mind, your thoughts and faith action have manifested your good.

If you have followed all of the phases to *Secrets of Prosperity*, such as making a commitment to implement the phases into your daily routine, then you will receive whatever it is that your heart desires. As you continue with your daily program, you will receive permanent prosperity and know a life that is second to none!

Your faith in action moves your ideas and aspirations forward. You could diligently work all of the steps to *Secrets* day in and day out, but if you do not believe you can receive, or do not attach faith to your Master Plan, then attainment of your good will likely be delayed.

> *Faith knows that uncertainty and trepidation is never ever permanent. Faith asks us to move beyond mere belief, and it asks us to step into the unknown, fearful or not.*

You can bring forth whatever it is that you desire. All things are formed through the action of the mind. It is through your thoughts and words that prosperity (or your daily abundance) waits for you in the ethers of the universe. It particularly waits for you to mold your good by deliberately shaping your thoughts to prosperous ones. It waits for you to create and design your mind and your words into that which you desire. The truth is, all you have to do is claim and accept your true abundance and it shall be delivered unto you. You have the power through thought, mind, and action to bring the conditions of your life into harmony and success.

You can contact the universal flow of substance into your life, which will manifest as your good, by speaking out loud what you wish or desire, attach the faith principle to it, imagine it, feel it, and you'll be over the rainbow!

Below is another affirmation that opens the channel of good to flow to you:

> *I welcome and accept the powerful substance of the universe into my life now. I claim my joy and success now.*

One of the most important things to remember is the following: You must gain an *inner feeling* of abundance before prosperity (or your aim, wish or dream) is given to you. Feel as though you have already received your good well in advance. This action precedes your demonstration, so hold to the inner truth and know that your blessings are already here. Expect to receive your gifts with joy and thanksgiving. The moment you deeply *feel* that your supplication is part of you, it is then that your manifestation or realization is right there for you to receive it. Expression or manifestation is another way of saying the result of the cause. All cause is implemented or brought about mentally. Your physical body, your affairs in your home, personal relationships and financial status are all manifestations of your mental state or thoughts.

State the following affirmations in order to help remove guilt from your mind:

I deserve my good.

There is no guilt.

All shame is now removed from me.

I accept and receive prosperity and abundance now.

I will maintain permanent abundance every minute of every day.

I do not strain or work hard in my endeavors, everything good now comes to me quickly and with ease.

Divine completion of my good is here. I love being over the rainbow.

Remember, faith moves substance forward. Be willing to receive with gratitude and thanksgiving. Always seal your good by making it spiritual and tithe ten percent of your income, time or talent. Moreover, bless what you have received, for whatever you bless always multiplies. Do not apologize for your good or for the wealth that you receive.

And when all else fails and you feel discouraged, change your attitude and give to others. Be still and listen to the still, small voice within, for therein lies the blessings of all life. Your life will change for the better if you take these two simple actions.

As your good continues to come forth, a new surge of energy will flow to you and you will receive a new inner source of strength, zeal and joy of life. New ideas and the ways and means to express those ideas will bubble up from within you to grant you unlimited abundance and permanent prosperity. Spirit will reveal to you your life purpose and your divine plan.

Engage in all of the steps that we have offered you. You can create the life that you want right here right now. The law of the divine tells us that if we already have a desire in our heart with a touch of faith it is given, and all you have to do is believe.

Notes on *Over the Rainbow*

Describe what landing in the pot of gold at the end of the rainbow looks like, smells like, sounds like, and feels like

____

____

____

____

____

At what point in your study of prosperity did you *feel* that you were already successful?

____

____

____

____

____

Maintaining Your Good

If the faith of a child could be bottled up and sold we would literally have heaven on earth.

Mary Beth Murawski

After you have received your good, or whatever you wrote down in Mission One, you must maintain the success that you have worked so vigorously to obtain. It is imperative that you continue to apply the daily principles and the missions of *Secrets of Prosperity*. Live and breathe each stage so that it naturally becomes part of you. Returning to old habits that are against the law of prosperity, at this point, would be counter productive. It is essential that you sustain your efforts and commit to applying the phases of *Secrets of Prosperity* vigilantly and without reservation. We have found that when you do receive your entitlement, it is a result of divine law in action. You now have completed the phases or steps to unlimited prosperity as outlined in our program.

Often, people have a tendency to become lazy or sluggish with the practice of their daily prosperity regime. Better yet, they become so comfortable in their newfound prosperity and abundance they feel that there is nothing else to do now that they are in the Eden state of mind. But the Eden state of mind takes constant vigilance to maintain. How do you stay over the rainbow?

Many people experience significant fear once their good arrives. They fear that they will lose all that they have gained. Fear of losing what you have is very common among truth seekers. Perhaps you find it difficult to receive your blessings. Or you fear that you might lose the new relationship, or that it might not work out. You got your dream job just as you wrote down in detail, but now fear you are not worthy. Do not listen to your lower fearful self. Begin taking action right away.

Affirm the following:

All fear is false. I have nothing to fear. My good is here and I claim it, accept it and receive it. God's good is permanent. There is nothing to fear.

If your good has not arrived, or you feel stuck in lack and limitation in one or more areas of your life, then fill this void with quiet listening. Be still and listen to the sacred place inside of you. The place that whispers gently to you in your time of need. Fill the void that you are experiencing with quiet contemplation inside your sacred dominion. Just rest there quietly. Whatever is lacking in your life will be filled as you replace this limitation or lack with love. The moment you switch your thoughts to love all lack and limitation will be removed. Success is your only option when you go to that secret place inside of yourself and live in love.

Perhaps one of your main goals is to be safe and comfortable in all areas of your life. This goal feels wonderful when accomplished. However, in order to maintain your new comfort zone, remember the daily mental missions to sustain your prosperity and abundance.

Do not give up on doing your daily missions and do not end your commitments, not even for a day. Go back to your Master Plan that you wrote down. Ask yourself is there anything that I still want in my life? Revise your Master Plan to create more aspirations and goals. Make amendments and changes as needed. Go back to Mission One and read your *Writing From The Heart* daily pages. Ask yourself, "Is there anything missing?" And then start all over again.

Most people enjoy the new experience of using their creative imagination to recognize success. However, if you find it tedious or you become impatient, view your flash cards, write it down again, live in your daily affirmations, give to others and stay positive. You will be back on track before you know it. When all else fails, create another vacuum and at the same time ask yourself who do you need to forgive? And then forgive without reservation.

Rejoice in all of your blessings and continue to act and breathe in faith daily. Remember:

> *Faith softens and erases particles of doubt that remind us of our ability to be human.*
>
> *Feel the prosperity and abundance from within...as within, so without.*

Notes on *Maintaining Your Good*

Doodle Space

Conclusion

Your *good* or dreams, desires and goals have been delivered via divine law and divine guidance because:

1. You knew what you wanted in every area of your life and then wrote it down in exact detail, with clarity, and pure intention. You also put a date down in writing when you wanted to receive your dream or heart's desire.
2. You created flash cards and pin-up phrases that depicted the precise visual images (from magazines and photograph) describing an itemized, detailed account of what you wanted and reviewed your flash cards and pin-ups at least twice daily. You did this upon arising in the morning and just before retiring at night.
3. Through the power of words you wrote your own affirmations, or you used the ones offered in *Secrets of Prosperity* Boot Camp, by making a formal declaration aloud that verbally asked for your desires, goals, dreams or wishes. This was done by speaking aloud and affirming through words exactly what you wanted. You repeated this daily, always attaching to your words faith and focused imagination. You learned to feel the words through your emotional nature, which supported the rapid manifestation of your *good*.
4. You practiced the *Kahuna* Prayer daily, changing negative belief systems and deeply embedded negative patterns from your conscious mind and re-created new prosperous abundant and healthy thoughts with the power of breath to your higher or subconscious self. This prayer

was repeated several times daily (in the morning and the evening until results appeared). You removed guilt, shame, fear, and resentment during the *Kahuna* prayer. This task became easier and easier as you imagined your "good" into physical reality.

5. You created a *Physical, Mental, and Social Vacuum* to remove all clutter and chaos form your physical surroundings as well as your mind.

6. You not only forgave yourself as well as others, but also successfully learned how to practice focused acts of forgiveness on a daily basis. These acts of forgiveness opened a channel for even greater good to come to you. People around you noticed that something had changed inside of you. They could not quite put their finger on it. You experienced a magnificent transformation in attitude and outlook upon everything. You were different in a beautiful way. Perhaps you understood the meaning of peace for the first time in your life. You forgave everybody and everything, without reservation.

7. You discovered how to give what you did not have and gave to yourself and others without reservation or conditions. This opened the way for you to feel worthy and to receive whatever you wrote down as your dreams, goals and desires began to come to you. Receiving your good or your demonstration became effortless as you leaped with joy to the other side of the rainbow. You expected your good to manifest, and it did. You called it forth and it happened.

8. Although difficult at times, you arduously completed the thirty-day *Mental Fast*, whereby every thought, word and action was derived from your mind and heart out of love. Success was now yours for the taking. Patience, joy, success, kindness, unlimited wealth, abundance, health, and peace filled your mind, body and soul. At this point, your life took a dramatic shift upward toward realizing your dreams. Synchronistic events came to you form the *ethers*

of the universe and divine guidance touched you in every area of your life. Ideas now became truth as long as it did not harm others. You began to believe that anything was possible, anything. You felt brand new. Miraculous events surrounded you and those around you. You started to feel lighter and the word "hope" made you excited. Wishes and dreams of long standing came to you effortlessly and with ease.

9. You gave of your time talent, energy and money to your place of spiritual fulfillment. You gladly tithed ten percent or more of your income. It came back to you seventy-seven fold. Your mere act of tithing sealed your prosperity and made it permanent. You gave praise and thanksgiving to God even before your good was delivered. Always, always faith gently moved you into your right place or toward your hearts desire.

10. Then, seemingly all of sudden, things shifted and appeared to fall apart. You experienced the convergence or the chemical break down between your conscious and subconscious mind. Nevertheless, you held on in faith during your convergence. The kind of faith that would accept nothing but the desire of your heart. Your eyes, mind and heart looked up toward your *aims* despite challenges, difficulties and blocks. You learned valuable lessons. Mistakes were turned into priceless experience that inevitable benefited you. You did not make major changes in your life during this time and you were gentle with yourself. You persisted with courage in the daily application of practicing all of the phases of *Secrets of Prosperity*. Most importantly, you did not give up. Some of you acquired courage and wisdom during this stage.

11. And then your good appeared according to divine law. And according to the thoughts, words and actions that you took, now became a part of you. Everything that you wrote down in Mission One became a celebration as you enjoyed the fruits of your expression or your good. Once again,

you glided into your right and perfect place *Over The Rainbow.* You gave praise and thanksgiving back to God for delivering your dreams. And you began to feel that every morning was Christmas and every night was Thanksgiving. Happiness, joy, unlimited wealth, daily abundance, perfect health, patience and success surround you. It stuck like a magnet. You felt it inside of your secret place and knew it would never be taken away. Therefore, you boldly shared your *Secrets of Prosperity* with others gladly as part of giving back to the universe. You played it forward. Your good or your demonstration was sealed and made permanent because you continued to implement every phase of *Secrets of Prosperity* daily for the rest of your prosperous life.

You realized that by changing yourself you could then participate in changing the world for the better. You now know how successful people receive their success so humbly. They expected it. They visualized it. Rehearsed it and felt it!

Congratulations!
You graduated from Boot Camp!

Please play it forward and share your secrets to prosperity by acting as an angel to your friends, family and the world.

Gracefully,
Jaime and Mary Beth

Mary Beth Murawski

Poet, writer, speaker and lover of life. Mary Beth is a natural in the communication of abundance and the power of love. She was born and raised in Ipswich, Massachusetts. As a child, her grandfather preached Norman Vincent Peal, and read to her from *The Power of Positive Thinking*, at age eleven. As a celebrated athlete, coupled with her passion for horses, Mary Beth finds joy in riding, coaching field hockey, and in practicing equine massage. In rock solid faith, Mary Beth walks her talk in mind, body and spirit – moving her life forward in prayer.

Jaime J. Harris

Writer, director, speaker and teacher is a Gemini in the purest sense. Many of the mission steps described in *Secrets* were developed while coaching actors in the Broadway and off Broadway theatre scene in New York City. Her study of mind science includes bio-feedback, neuro linguistics programming and hypnotherapy. Incorporating all of these techniques and combining life and work experiences, eventually led Ms.Harris to create and develop the basis of precepts used in *Secrets of Prosperity*. She is currently working on a novel of fiction and resides on Prince Edward Island.